T0059535

CARMEN OLIVER

LUISA URIBE

# BUILDING AN ORCHESTRA OF HOPE

## HOW FAVIO CHÁVEZ TAUGHT CHILDREN TO MAKE MUSIC FROM TRASH

EERDMANS BOOKS FOR YOUNG READERS

GRAND RAPIDS, MICHIGAN

As a young child, Favio sang in the choir and played guitar. Music was the first thing that gave him a sense of purpose. But years later, after studying environmental science, his purpose shifted. Now he was headed to Cateura, Paraguay— a small village built on a landfill—to try to help the families who lived and worked amid the hills of trash.

Every day, he watched trucks dump
load after load. The trash weighed
more than a herd of elephants.
1500 tons!

Glass clinked. Metal pinged. Plastic bags rustled.
The recyclers, called gancheros, filled their bags to the top.
They survived by collecting and reselling garbage.
They breathed a sea of stench. They waded through filth.
"It is not a place where people are supposed to live," Favio said.

But people did.

It was backbreaking labor to swing
handmade hoes all day long.
Gancheros ripped through bags,
foraging for anything they could sell.
Five cents a pound for cardboard.
Ten cents a pound for plastic.

Favio supervised the gancheros and became friends with them and their children. He worried about the kids' futures. Would they end up working in the landfill like their parents?

After working long days at the landfill, Favio
conducted a youth orchestra in a nearby village.
One day his ganchero friends came to watch him.

The music captivated their hearts.

Could their children be taught how to play instruments?

Favio thought so—and he'd be honored to teach them!

Favio brought his own guitars and violins to the landfill.

At the lessons, the children sat on overturned crates and barrels.

Before long, Favio had a serious problem.

He had more kids than instruments.
What was he going to do?

Favio didn't want to turn any child away.
But instruments were expensive.
A violin cost more than a house in Cateura.
He could raise money to purchase a few
instruments for the children,
but that posed another problem.

A much more serious problem.

Most homes in Cateura were built from recycled tin, metal, and wood from the landfill. Many didn't have plumbing or electricity.

The rivers around Cateura were contaminated. People walked on foot. Or biked. Only a few owned motorcycles or cars.

Expensive instruments in homes would entice thieves, putting families in danger.

No, Favio couldn't risk that.
He needed to come up with a better solution.

But what?

One day at the landfill, Favio watched his ganchero friend Nicolás "Colá" Gómez picking trash.

Colá was an innovative carpenter, which gave Favio an idea.

He told Colá his plan.

Then he watched Colá comb through scrap heaps, looking for anything he could use to make instruments.

Colá collected oven trays, old drain pipes,
door keys, metal forks and spoons, X-ray films,
bottle caps, glue canisters, plastic buttons,
paint cans, wooden crates, and oil barrels.
Every day, he carried his treasures home to
his woodworking shop.

Favio asked Colá to make a violin.
Colá borrowed Favio's violin to get precise
measurements. A picture formed in Colá's mind,
and he went to work.

Colá built his first violin.
The body was cut from a metal commercial glue canister
covered with Portuguese writing and symbols.
A wooden spoon and door keys held the strings in place.
The bow was constructed from recycled wood.
Favio and Colá beamed. It was a thing of beauty.
But how would it sound?

It wasn't pitch-perfect. But it was a
great first attempt.

Favio taught the children how to play music on this new instrument.

He taught them how to hold the bow at the right angle.

He taught them how to hold the violin under their chin.

He taught them how to read notes.

"You're going to make mistakes," he said.
"But don't let that upset you."

After practice was over, Favio asked Colá
for a few more favors.

Over several years, Colá made a drum with X-ray films as drumheads, a viola from a paint can, flutes and saxophones from drain pipes, a cello from an oil barrel, and a trumpet with worthless coins serving as valve caps.

Finally, Favio had enough instruments for every child who wanted to learn how to make music. And what music they made!

In a vacated school yard, Favio taught thirty children how to play their recycled instruments, and how to read music. It was a huge accomplishment because many of the children didn't even know how to read words.

During the rainy season, they shuffled into the
deserted classrooms, and Favio conducted.
They practiced and practiced and practiced.
Finally, the time came to perform for their parents,
who had never heard the children play.

A local church served
as the grand stage.

Early in the day, the children
swept the dirt floors.

They carried in chairs.

They had an informal dress rehearsal,
then went home to change, returning
in their finest clothes.

Parents packed the modest place of worship.
The notes to "New York, New York" floated out
the windows and into the warm night air.

Parents shed happy tears.
The parents and their children had only been concerned
about surviving the next day. But now they had hope in
their hearts and dreams for a better tomorrow.

"The world sends us garbage," Favio says.
"We send back music."

# MORE ABOUT FAVIO CHÁVEZ AND THE RECYCLED ORCHESTRA OF CATEURA

## Cateura, Paraguay

Tucked away in the middle of the continent of South America is the country of Paraguay. It shares its borders with the countries of Bolivia, Brazil, and Argentina. Paraguay's capital city, Asunción, is home to about three million people. Every day trucks depart Asunción and trek seven miles along dirt roads to dump 1500 tons of garbage in the Cateura landfill. The tiny town of Cateura is built in a flood zone around this mountain of garbage.

From sunup to sundown, squawking birds and sweating gancheros pick through trash in the sweltering heat. While the gancheros work, the children too young for school play in homemade swings of plastic cables tied to trees. When school lets out, their siblings join them in searching for treasure in the towering rubble. They find everything from gold jewelry to vinyl records to Coca-Cola signs. Cateura is a city ripe for dreams. Ripe for hope. As Favio says, "We must never stop dreaming."

## I Want To Be A Part of It

Favio Hernán Chávez Morán was born in Buenos Aires, Argentina, on December 5, 1975. At a young age, he and his family moved to Carapeguá, Paraguay. Favio attended school, sang in the church choir, and learned to play guitar there. After graduating from high school in 1993, he studied engineering and human ecology at the National University of Asunción. He also developed his music studies at the Asunción Municipal Institute of Art.

In 2006, Favio arrived to work on a recycling project at the Cateura landfill. His job was to educate the people there about better ways to collect and sort garbage. When he wasn't supervising the gancheros, he was teaching their kids how to play music. Soon, he had more kids than instruments. It occurred to Favio that more instruments could be made out of trash. He asked Colá, one of the gancheros, who was also a skilled carpenter, to construct the first violin. "What struck me from the start was that this man [Colá] never thought about financial gain," Favio said later. With Colá's ingenuity, they created an entire orchestra of instruments made from the trash. Favio called it the Recycled Orchestra of Cateura.

In 2009, Alejandra Amarilla Nash, a Paraguayan born in Asunción, heard about the orchestra. She dreamed of helping her homeland through creativity, so she and her team decided to produce the documentary film *Landfill Harmonic*, starring some of the child musicians and Favio, the director and heart of the orchestra.

## Start Spreading the News

Once the documentary trailer surfaced on the internet, offers from around the globe started pouring in for the orchestra to perform. In 2012, Favio found himself helping his young musicians purchase shirts, luggage, and secure government documents to travel to their first international concert in Rio de Janeiro, Brazil. For many of the the children, this was their first time flying in an airplane or staying in a hotel or even seeing the ocean. Favio encouraged them to help each other, not only by learning the music but also by being good friends to one another. They needed to think as a team, not as individuals.

Today, the orchestra has performed in many countries including Argentina, Canada, Spain, Brazil, Japan, and the United States. They have played with rock bands like Megadeth and Metallica, as well as entertained dignitaries like Queen Sofía of Spain and Pope Francis!

## Little Town Blues

In 2014, after days of rain, the Paraguay River swelled, spilling its banks and flooding Cateura. Families lost everything and had to abandon their homes, moving into makeshift refugee camp structures of plywood and plastic. A few miles away in Asunción, Favio worked tirelessly to find temporary homes for the kids and their families. To avoid living in the unsafe streets of Cateura, many stayed at the music school in Asunción where Favio taught the students. Finally, two and a half months later, the floods receded and allowed some families to return to their homes and begin rebuilding.

In 2017, orchestra musicians and their families who had been affected by the floods moved into new homes in Bañado Sur, Asunción. These homes were built in a joint project between the Recycled Orchestra of Cateura and Habitat for Humanity Paraguay. Now, plans are underway to build more homes for orchestra families. The money came from donations and money earned in concerts.

## Make A Brand New Start of It

In April 2018, the Recycled Orchestra of Cateura participated in a charity concert in Spain and earned money to help build a community health center in Bañado Sur. The orchestra has also worked to bring more art and culture into the area with mosaics splashed on building walls. During the COVID-19 pandemic, the orchestra supported families with food, aid, and computer equipment so kids could focus on their schoolwork.

Today, the Recycled Orchestra of Cateura pushes forward with scholarships and many humanitarian efforts. They work to make connections between different worlds and improve the lives of those who live and breathe and make music in Paraguay. As Favio has said: "Music is the bridge."

# SELECTED BIBLIOGRAPHY

### First Person

Chávez, Favio. Email correspondence with Carmen Oliver. 2021 to present.

### Websites

Orquesta de Reciclados de Cateura (Recycled Orchestra of Cateura). 2014. recycledorchestracateura.com.

*Landfill Harmonic*. Meetai Films, et al., 2022. landfillharmonicmovie.com.

### Videos

Chávez, Favio, "The World Sends Us Garbage, We Send Back Music: Favio Chávez at TEDxAmsterdam." YouTube Video. Nov. 8, 2013. https://www.youtube.com/watch?v=CsfOvJEdurk&t=87s.

Dupps, Dennis, "Landfill Harmonic Amazing and Inspirational," YouTube Video. July 10, 2014. https://www.youtube.com/watch?v=4D9Y4WFFcSw.

Simon, Bob, correspondent, "The Recyclers: From Trash Comes Triumph." *60 Minutes*, CBS. New York: CBS News, November 17, 2013, and May 11, 2014. Paramount Plus. https://www.cbsnews.com/news/recyclers-from-trash-comes-triumph-2/.

### Articles

Bunn, Susan Drennan Gabriel. "Musician Hero: Favio Chávez." My Hero, January 6, 2017. https://myhero.com/Favio_Chavez_2013.

Crasta, Ranjan. "This Orchestra From the Slums Turns Hopelessness to Harmony." CatchNews, Sept. 22, 2016. http://www.catchnews.com/life-society-news/this-orchestra-from-the-slums-turns-hopelessness-to-harmony-1474486079.html.

Greer, Carlos. "Favio Chávez Helps Children Make Music—Out of Trash." *People*, May 9, 2013. https://people.com/human-interest/musicians-brings-hope-to-kids-living-in-slums-in-paraguay/.

Horton, Robin Plaskoff. "Youth Orchestra's Instruments All Made From Recycled Landfill Trash." Urban Gardens, July 22, 2013. https://www.urbangardensweb.com/2013/07/22/youth-orchestras-instruments-all-made-from-recycled-landfill-trash/.

Laksman, Mariela. "From Garbage to Great Music." *Orato World Media*, April 6, 2021. https://orato.world/2021/04/06/from-garbage-to-great-music/.

Mashurova, Nina. "Landfill Harmonic: A Story of Creativity, Hope, and Endurance." Matador Network, December 12, 2012. https://matadornetwork.com/change/landfill-harmonic-a-story-of-creativity-hope-and-endurance-interview/.

Ramdane, Ines. "From Trash to Tchaikovsky." *USA Today*, June 25, 2015. https://www.usatoday.com/story/news/world/2015/06/25/impact-journalism-day-from-trash-to-tchaikovsky/29287107/.

Tsioulcas, Anastasia. "The Landfill Harmonic: An Orchestra Built From Trash" NPR, December 19, 2012. http://www.npr.org/blogs/deceptivecadence/2012/12/19/167539764/the-landfill-harmonic-an-orchestra-built-from-trash.

For Marjorie and the Charlotte S. Huck Children's Literature Festival: thank you for creating a culture steeped in stories, where children's book creators & educators can thrive.

And for Favio, the Recycled Orchestra of Cateura, and their families: thank you for letting us be a small part of your musical journey and legacy of hope.

— C. O.

Para Ana María y Bernardo, con cariño.

— L. U.

## SOURCES

"It is not a place . . . " Chávez, Favio, qtd. in Greer, Carlos, "Favio Chávez Helps Children Make Music–Out of Trash," *People*, May 9, 2013, https://people.com/human-interest/musicians-brings-hope-to-kids-living-in-slums-in-paraguay/.

"You're going . . . " Chávez, Favio, qtd. in *Landfill Harmonic*, dir. by Brad Allgood and Graham Townsley (Los Angeles: The Film Collaborative, 2015). Film.

"The world sends . . . " Ibid.

"We must never . . . " Ibid.

"What really struck me . . . " Chávez, Favio, qtd. in Dennis Drupps, "Landfill Harmonic Amazing and Inspirational," YouTube Video, 11:44, July 10, 2014, https://youtu.be/4D9Y4WFFcSw.

" . . . music is the bridge." Ibid.

Text © 2022 Carmen Oliver
Illustrations © 2022 Luisa Uribe

Published in 2022 by
Eerdmans Books for Young Readers
an imprint of Wm. B. Eerdmans Publishing Co.
Grand Rapids, Michigan

www.eerdmans.com/youngreaders

All rights reserved

Manufactured in the United States of America

31 30 29 28 27 26 25 24 23 22      1 2 3 4 5 6 7 8 9

Illustrations created digitally

**Library of Congress Cataloging-in-Publication Data**

Names: Oliver, Carmen, author. | Uribe, Luisa, illustrator.
Title: Building an orchestra of hope : how Favio Chávez taught children to make music from trash / Carmen Oliver, Luisa Uribe.
Description: Grand Rapids, Michigan : Eerdmans Books for Young Readers, 2022. | Audience: Ages 4 - 9 | Summary: "When a children's orchestra in Cateura, Paraguay, grows to have more students than instruments, music teacher Favio Chávez works with a brilliant local carpenter to create instruments out of garbage from the local landfill"— Provided by publisher.
Identifiers: LCCN 2022000480 | ISBN 9780802854674 (hardcover) | ISBN 9781467465908 (ebook)
Subjects: LCSH: Chávez, Favio—Juvenile literature. | Orquesta de Instrumentos Reciclados Cateura—Juvenile literature. | Music teachers—Paraguay—Biography—Juvenile literature. | LCGFT: Biographies. | Picture books.
Classification: LCC ML3930.C446 O45 2022 | DDC 780.71/02 [B]—dc23
LC record available at https://lccn.loc.gov/2022000480

We wish to thank Favio Chávez for his feedback on this story, and for granting permission for the use of his name and that of the Recycled Orchestra.

Those wishing to learn more or make donations to the orchestra can contact the Association of Parents of the Orchestra of Recycled Instruments of Cateura.

www.facebook.com/asopadresorquestacateura/

www.instagram.com/aso_padres_cateura/